MY COMMUNITY

A TRIP TO THE CONSTRUCTION SITE

Nora Ellison

PowerKiDS press.

New York

Published in 2017 by The Rosen Publishing Group, Inc.
29 East 21st Street, New York, NY 10010

First Edition

Editor: Melissa Raé Shofner
Book Design: Mickey Harmon

Photo Credits: Cover Ariel Skelley/Getty Images; p. 5 Darryl Brooks/Shutterstock.com; p. 6 bikeriderlondon/Shutterstock.com; p. 9 michaeljung/Shutterstock.com; p. 10 Dmitry Kalinovsky/Shutterstock.com; p. 13 TFoxFoto/Shutterstock.com; p. 17 Mirko Rosenau/Shutterstock.com; p. 18 Dan70/Shutterstock.com; p. 21 gpointstudio/Shutterstock.com; p. 22 Bloomberg/Contributor/Bloomberg/Getty Images.

Cataloging-in-Publication Data

Names: Ellison, Nora.
Title: A Trip to the construction site / Nora Ellison.
Description: New York : PowerKids Press, 2017. | Series: My community | Includes index.
Identifiers: ISBN 9781499427806 (pbk.) | ISBN 9781499430042 (library bound) | ISBN 9781508152934 (6 pack)
Subjects: LCSH: Building–Juvenile literature. | Building sites–Juvenile literature. | Construction workers–Juvenile literature. | Construction equipment–Juvenile literature.
Classification: LCC TH375.E45 2017 | DDC 690–d23

Manufactured in the United States of America

CPSIA Compliance Information: Batch #BW17PK: For Further Information contact Rosen Publishing, New York, New York at 1-800-237-9932

CONTENTS

A house is being built.

The boss has the plans.

Everyone wears a **hardhat**.
Safety first!

A digger makes a hole.

A **truck** moves the dirt.

Pipes go in the ground.

Workers build the walls.

They use saws to make boards shorter.

They use hammers and nails.

The house is almost done.

WORDS TO KNOW

hardhat

pipes

truck

INDEX

WEBSITES

Due to the changing nature of Internet links, PowerKids Press has developed an online list of websites related to the subject of this book. This site is updated regularly. Please use this link to access the list: www.powerkidslinks.com/mycom/construc